DATE DUE AR 4.2

FEB 2 2 2000			

Making Their Mark: Women in Sports™

Gabrielle Reece
Star Volleyball Player

Liza N. Burby

The Rosen Publishing Group's
PowerKids Press™
New York

Published in 1997 by The Rosen Publishing Group, Inc.
29 East 21st Street, New York, NY 10010

First Edition

Book Design: Erin McKenna

Photo Credits: cover and pp. 4, 11, 15, 16, 19, 20 © Michael Zito/Sportschrome East/West; p. 7 © Eberhard Otto/FPG International Corp; p. 8 © J. Zimmerman/FPG International Corp.; p. 12 by Kim M. Sonsky.

Burby, Liza N.
    Gabrielle Reece, star volleyball player/ by Liza N. Burby
        p.   cm. — (Making their mark)
    Includes index.
    Summary: Discusses the life and achievements of the award-winning professional volleyball star who also shines as a fashion model, basketball player, magazine writer, and television personality.
    ISBN 0-8239-5067-0
    1. Reece, Gabrielle—Juvenile literature. 2. Volleyball players—United States—Biography—Juvenile literature. [1. Reece, Gabrielle. 2. Volleyball players 3. Women—Biography.]
    I. Series: Burby, Liza N. Making their mark.
GV1015.26.R44B87 1997
796.325'092—dc21
                                                                                96-41730
                                                                                    CIP
                                                                                    AC

Manufactured in the United States of America

Contents

1   An Independent Girl   5

2   A New Home   6

3   Discovering Sports   9

4   Hard Work and Practice   10

5   Becoming a Model   13

6   A Leader in Volleyball   14

7   Star of the Beach   17

8   Strong and Beautiful   18

9   A Popular Sport   21

10   Gabrielle Likes Volleyball Best   22

     Glossary   23

     Index   24

An Independent Girl

Gabrielle Reece was born on January 6, 1970 in La Jolla, California. Gabrielle was an **independent** (IN-dee-PEN-dent) little girl. In many ways she had to be. Gabrielle was only two years old when her mother, a dolphin trainer for the circus, decided that she couldn't take care of Gabrielle. Her parents were **divorced** (dih-VORST) and Gabrielle wasn't able to live with her father. So she went to live with her mother's friends in New York. Gabrielle stayed there for five years.

◄ Gabrielle learned at a very young age to take care of herself.

A New Home

Gabrielle was seven when she moved back in with her mother. But Gabrielle was not happy. She was angry about having to leave the family in New York that had taken care of her. Gabrielle did not always listen to what her mother told her to do. She and her mother had a lot of arguments.

During that time, Gabrielle's mother remarried. She and Gabrielle moved in with Gabrielle's new stepfather on the island of St. Thomas in the U.S. Virgin Islands.

St. Thomas is the second largest of six ▶ islands in the U.S. Virgin Islands.

Discovering Sports

Gabrielle was very tall for her age. By the time she was fifteen years old, she was six-feet, three inches tall. Her height made her feel different from the other kids at school. Following the advice of some of her classmates and teachers, Gabrielle played on the school basketball and volleyball teams. Her height helped the teams win more games.

Gabrielle started to like playing these sports. She learned that playing sports helped her feel good about herself.

◄ Like many teen girls, Gabrielle enjoyed playing sports in high school. They made her feel more confident.

Hard Work and Practice

Gabrielle was a good player. She and her team made it to the state finals in basketball. Several colleges wanted her to play on their college basketball teams. But Gabrielle chose to play volleyball instead when the coach from Florida State University offered her a volleyball **scholarship** (SKAH-ler-ship).

With hard work and practice, Gabrielle became the top **blocker** (BLOK-er) at her university. She was also very good at **kills** (KILZ).

A kill in volleyball is when a player hits the ball over the net very hard. ▶

Becoming a Model

When Gabrielle was in college, someone asked her if she wanted to be a **model** (MAH-dul). She decided to try it. The first time Gabrielle modeled only her hands. She earned a lot of money. She also thought modeling was fun. So Gabrielle started spending half of the year playing volleyball and the other half modeling. She appeared in famous **fashion** (FA-shun) magazines, such as *Italian Vogue* and *Elle*.

◀ Gabrielle is seen in many fashion and fitness magazines.

13

A Leader in Volleyball

Gabrielle really enjoyed playing volleyball. She said that volleyball made her feel good about herself. When she was twenty, Gabrielle was named the All-Southeastern Conference middle blocker. She is still the all-time leading blocker for Florida State University. In 1993, she went to California to play doubles beach volleyball. This is a game played with two people on each team. Gabrielle says she did not play well on this team. She was used to playing with four people per team. But she didn't give up.

Gabrielle prefers to play on teams of four people. ▶

Star of the Beach

Gabrielle decided to stay in California and work hard to strengthen her body. She was asked to be on a volleyball **circuit** (SIR-kut) of four-woman teams. She was the first woman picked, and she also was named captain of the team in the Pro Beach Volleyball **League** (LEEG).

In 1994, Gabrielle was given awards for Best Player and Most Improved Player. She had become the star of the beach.

◀ Being the best is not easy. Gabrielle worked hard to get to where she is in volleyball.

17

Strong and Beautiful

Gabrielle was becoming a famous athlete. Nike, a sporting goods company, asked Gabrielle to help design a sneaker. So she helped to create the Air Trainer Patrol sneaker for women. Then she appeared in TV **commercials** (kuh-MER-shulz) to show that women's sports can be exciting. For a long time, people thought that women should not play sports. But with the help of athletes like Gabrielle, people are now seeing that women can be star **athletes** (ATH-leets) in professional sports.

Gabrielle showed everyone that women can be strong, athletic, and beautiful. ▶

A Popular Sport

Not everyone agrees with what Gabrielle does. Some say she is only famous as an athlete because she is a famous model too. But Gabrielle says that she works hard as a volleyball player.

Gabrielle has made volleyball very popular. Doubles beach volleyball was played in the Olympics for the first time in 1996 in Atlanta, Georgia. Gabrielle hopes that volleyball teams of four will be in the 2000 Olympics so she can play this too!

◀ Gabrielle gives everything she's got to each practice and game.

Gabrielle Likes Volleyball Best

Today, Gabrielle does not model as much as she used to. She wants to have more time for volleyball. Gabrielle writes about **fitness** (FIT-nes) for *Elle*, a women's magazine, and has had her own sports TV shows. But playing volleyball is what she loves best. Gabrielle says she does everything else just for fun. She says it is important for her to show people that as a woman you can be a great athlete and you can be strong.

Glossary

athlete (ATH-leet) A person who plays sports.

blocker (BLOK-er) A player who stops another team from getting a point.

circuit (SIR-kut) A group of teams that play against each other.

commercial (kuh-MER-shul) A message on the radio or TV before or during programs that sells something.

divorce (dih-VORS) The legal ending of a marriage.

fashion (FA-shun) Clothes and styles that people like.

fitness (FIT-nes) Being healthy and strong.

independent (IN-dee-PEN-dent) Thinking for or taking care of oneself.

kills (KILZ) When a player hits the ball over the net so hard that the other team can't stop it.

league (LEEG) A group of teams.

model (MAH-dul) A person who has his or her picture taken for magazines.

scholarship (SKAH-ler-ship) Money set aside to pay for a student-athlete's education once he or she has agreed to play for that school's team.

Index

A
athletes, 18, 22

B
blocks, 10

C
circuit, 17
colleges, 10, 13,
    14
commercials, 18

F
fashion, 13
fitness, 22

I
independent, 5

K
kills, 10

L
leagues, 17

M
magazines, 13,
    22
modeling, 13, 21,
    22

N
Nike, 18

O
Olympics, 21

S
scholarship, 10
sports, 9
  playing, 9, 18

T
teams, 14, 17,
    21